THE JOURNEY OF
DIEGO
RIVERA

THE JOURNEY OF
DIEGO RIVERA

ERNEST GOLDSTEIN

LERNER PUBLICATIONS COMPANY
MINNEAPOLIS

To Doctors David Carmichael, David Cohen, and George Todd, to whom
the oaths of Hippocrates and Maimonides represent the sacred calling.
L'amitié de l'âme comme dit l'autre.

And to my three muses, Marsha Cohen, Jenny Hart, and Natalie
Galen, who propped me up and would not permit me to fall.

The making of a juvenile art book requires expertise on many levels. The
author is thankful to those who made this book possible. The author
wishes to thank Harry Lerner for his vision, Sandy Davis for her insight,
Mary Winget for her editorial direction, Lynn Olsen for her help with the
visuals, and the staff of Lerner Publications Company.

Technical consultation for design: Zachary Marell and Robert Saunders

**92
RIV**

LIBRARY OF CONGRESS CATALOGING-IN-PUBLICATION DATA
Goldstein, Ernest, 1933–
  The journey of Diego Rivera / by Ernest Goldstein.
    p. cm.
  Includes index.
  Summary: Suggests ways to look at the murals and other paintings of this
twentieth-century Mexican artist while also indicating development of his style and
offering some biographical information.
  ISBN 0-8225-2066-4 (acid-free paper)
  1. Rivera, Diego, 1886–1957—Themes, motives—Juvenile literature. 2. Rivera,
Diego, 1886–1957—Psychology—Juvenile literature. [1. Rivera, Diego, 1886–1957.
2. Artists. 3. Mural painting and decoration—Mexico. 4. Painting, Mexican. 5. Art
appreciation.]
I. Rivera, Diego, 1886–1957. II. Title.
ND259.R5G66 1996
759.972—dc20   95-8163

Manufactured in the United States of America
1 2 3 4 5 6 - JR - 01 00 99 98 97 96

CONTENTS

CHAPTER ONE

BONAMPAK

You are about to join one of the world's most celebrated artists on a fantastic journey through time. Along the way you will encounter dazzling images of a long-forgotten past, images of one of the world's most important civilizations that will come alive again on a country's public walls and buildings.

We begin our journey, not with the artist, but by going to the thickest part of the Mexican jungle, near the equator, to a place called Bonampak. Bonampak had been hidden for centuries in the thick jungle of Chiapas and was believed to exist only as a legend among the prospectors and hunters of the region. But in 1947, this mythical kingdom was discovered to be an actual place still in existence. Bonampak, as described by writer Bradley Smith, is the *tierra caliente*—"a steamy, hot jungle of rivers, lagoons, and swamps where heavy

rains flood the countryside seasonally." Anyone who has ever seen Bonampak is overwhelmed by the magnificence of the frescoes on the walls of its ancient buildings. Scholars have compared the Bonampak frescoes to the frescoes by Michelangelo in the Sistine Chapel. In both locations, the walls of the buildings seem to exist for one purpose only—to exhibit the paintings that are on them. The relationship between art and architecture is so close that the frescoes seem to have been painted to conform to the abstract lines of the buildings. The art of Bonampak is sophisticated far beyond its time and place.

In the first room, we become aware of the visual conventions of the Bonampak artists by the use of parasols to direct the viewer's eye. Musicians frame the wall, making a border of sound that resembles the visual frame of the parasols.

Detail of mural from Mayan ruins at Bonampak, Room 1

Bonampak, Detail of Room 1

A group of five characters is performing a symbolic dance. Members of the group are wearing masks representing crabs, lizards, or perhaps iguanas.

What this scene means is not clear. Some scholars and writers have suggested various possibilities. It might be a religious occasion or a gathering of nobles. Others suggest an event that extends to the additional rooms—an event celebrating the great battles of a war, or ceremonies related to water. Maybe the mural represents a ceremony dedicated to a rain god, a ceremony that starts with the offering of an infant, continues with a battle to capture slaves, and ends with a celebration. Perhaps the mural represents the birth of a famous king or the great events of his victorious life.

Although the meaning may be unclear to contemporary viewers, the art of Bonampak has

Bonampak, Detail of Room 2
Warriors raiding a village to capture prisoners to be used for human sacrifice

a well-developed artistic maturity. This exquisite series of wall frescoes represents the flourishing Mayan civilization (A.D. 250–900). While Attila the Hun was laying Europe to waste and the Visigoths were sacking Rome, the primitive artists of Bonampak were creating extraordinary art. These paintings have a great freedom in design. The sense of movement created in that first room is unequalled in other "primitive" art. Although all the figures are in profile, they differ from each other in the subtle movements of the bodies and hands when playing the various instruments or engaged in conversation. There is a rhythm to their movements, a rhythm to the scene, a rhythm created by the music that fills in the space around these figures.

But there is much more to consider, so let us go into the second room. Here is a scene that probably depicts the aftermath of a battle, and it portrays prisoners being taken to use as slaves. Look at this scene closely. Most scholars who have written about this scene claim that one of the slaves is pleading for his life, a second has had his fingernails removed, and a third may have been beheaded. Most critics see this as a bloody scene—most, but not all!

The scholar Antonio Rodríguez notes the delicacy and refinement of Mayan civilization. He tells us that the Maya had little desire to change the order of things by creating unnecessary destruction or by mass slaughters. He cites the Mayan hunter who apologized to the game he was about to kill by saying "Otzilan," meaning "I need it."

According to Rodriguez, in the second chamber the painters of Bonampak produced a picture of a slave who was able to preserve his dignity even in the face of tragedy. When you look at him, you see a man whom nothing could defeat. In this representation of a slave, the Maya expressed a feeling for humanity that was characteristic of their art and life.

Bonampak, Detail of Room 2

CHAPTER TWO

THE ARTIST
ABROAD

Bonampak plays an important role in our story, but we must now jump in time to Paris in the year 1916. There, a young artist is about to show a major painting. Look at the work *Zapatista Landscape,* or *The Guerrilla. (Refer to page 18.)* Can you identify the painting, the technique or style, and the name of the artist?

If you had said Pablo Picasso, you would have agreed with most of the critics of the time. A major critic first responded to the work by saying, "Pablo Picasso's latest work is a masterpiece." Since it did resemble the works of Picasso, to mistake it was quite natural. The work was a cubist painting, and Picasso was the major cubist of the period. Looking at a cubist painting, the viewer tries to focus on an object. But the artist has painted the object from several angles and planes at the same time. The term for this is simultaneity. For the 1916 viewer, as well as today's viewer, the result is disarming.

With a cubist painting, you let your nose guide your eye. That's what Pablo Picasso said. "Looking at a cubist painting is like smelling a lovely odor of perfume." Where is it? Is it in front of you? Behind you? Or all around you? It moves. And it's that sense of vibrant movement that characterizes a cubist work.

Cubism is an attempt to combine three-dimensional sculpture and two-dimensional painting. You have to imagine walking around an object and piecing it together from several different sides in order to decide what the artist is trying to do.

Outskirts of Toledo, by Diego Rivera (1913)

Both El Greco's *View of Toledo* (c.1504), *left,* and Diego Rivera's *Landscape of Toledo* (1912), *on facing page,* depict the medieval city of Toledo, Spain, *above.* El Greco, however, chose to put the two main structures next to each other in his painting. Rivera retains their sense of distance.

Cubism, one of the great inventions of twentieth-century art, represents a major shift in the way artists present space. In 1916 it would not have been unreasonable to assume that Picasso had done this painting. But it is not his. It is the work of a young Mexican genius who had come to Paris to become part of the revolution called "modern art." His name: Diego Rivera.

Diego Rivera was born in Guanajuato, Mexico, in 1886. When he was 20 years old, he had shown so much talent that the Mexican government gave him a grant to go to Europe to study art. Europe, of course, had a long tradition in art. In the great museums, artists could study master-pieces of the past and carry on traditions in the workshops of famous art teachers. But Europe in 1905, especially Paris, was not the Europe of traditional art.

New movements and revolutions were changing the course of art for the rest of the world. Impressionism had already found its place, and now many other movements were emerging: post-impressionism, expressionism, pointillism, futurism, dadaism, constructivism, and, of course, cubism. Paris was the home of all these movements, and Diego Rivera found himself in the company of

the great artists and geniuses of the period. The list of his closest friends reads like a "Who's Who" in art—Pablo Picasso, Henri Matisse, and Amedeo Modigliani. For 14 years, Rivera traveled in Europe, studying the masterpieces of the past and gaining immense technical knowledge of modern art. During that time, his paintings began to reflect the wide range of his genius. When he went to Spain and studied the old master El Greco, he produced a series of paintings modeled after El Greco's masterpiece, *Toledo*. Rivera's *Toledo* shows the same view of Toledo as El Greco's, and it shows how Rivera changed forms in space to construct his image. In another painting of the period, *Outskirts of Toledo*, El Greco's influence, seen in the long figures of the old men, gives the painting a spiritual feeling.

In Rivera's *Notre Dame of Paris* (1909), you can see the influence of French impressionist Claude Monet. In this work, the solid church is softened and dissolved by mist so that the building and the atmosphere seem to come together in a burst of color and smoke. In still another landscape of Toledo, the colors suggest the influence of the famous artist Paul Cézanne.

Rivera's range was prodigious. His *Portrait of Aldolph Maugard* (1913) combines the style of El Greco with the colors of one of France's most famous modern painters, Robert Delaunay. Delaunay's school was known as Orphism, named after the Greek god Orpheus.

One more painting worth showing is Rivera's *Portrait of Martin Luis Guzman* (1915). Guzman lived in Mexico and had taken part in the Mexican Revolution. He was one of Mexico's most gifted writers and worked closely with the revolutionary hero Pancho Villa. Guzman's book, *The Eagle* *and the Serpent,* tells a chilling story about the horrors and cruelties done even by good men. When Guzman went to Paris, he spent much time with Rivera discussing revolutionary politics.

The subject of *Zapatista Landscape* is the revolution in Mexico. Living in Paris, the young Diego spent most of his time with fellow artists and revolutionaries sympathetic to the Mexican revolution. He had read closely *The Underdogs* by

Notre Dame of Paris,
by Diego Rivera (1909)

Portrait of Martin Luis Guzman,
by Diego Rivera (1915)

Mariano Azuela (1913). The novel describes the brutality and ferociousness of the Mexican Revolution. *Zapatista Landscape* suggests a rifle, a cartridge belt, a wooden box, a brightly colored Mexican serape, a sombrero of Emiliano Zapata (the folk hero who fought for justice for the Mexican laborers), and—in the background—a Mexican landscape of volcanoes and mountains.

The painting is full of cubist tricks. It shows a still life against a landscape floating in open space. The light sky is doubled in deep blue reflection below the horizon. The mountain landscape frames the hat above, while below, trees tip upside down into the blue. When you look at it, you are forced to think about what is real and what is imaginary, especially with *trompe l'oeil* (fool the eye)—a paper pinned to canvas on the painted nail. Rivera also uses dots of paint (pointillism) as decorations.

In this sophisticated painting, Rivera went one step beyond Picasso by introducing the rich colors of Mexico. For Picasso, cubism at this time meant design and line—not color. Objects were broken down into cubes and then came to life as parts of

Zapatista Landscape, by Diego Rivera (1915)

a composition. For Rivera, cubism meant taking separate objects and painting them in vibrant color, while the composition remained a polygon within the rectangle of canvas. The results were quite astonishing and brought Rivera to the very forefront of modern art in Europe.

With *Zapatista Landscape,* the artist, although living in Paris, could have been responding to the revolution going on in his homeland. And he was probably expressing memories of his adolescence in Mexico, as well as the homesickness of an expatriate in Paris.

Between 1905 and 1918, Rivera spent most of his time perfecting the techniques of modern art. Paris had become not only the center for the revolution known as modern art but also the intellectual center for Communist revolutions going on in Mexico and Russia. Rivera was on very close terms with revolutionary painters and writers. One of his closest friends, the Russian novelist Ilya Ehrenburg, was so taken by Rivera's charm and knowledge that he wrote a book on what it might have been like for young Diego Rivera in Mexico.

Throughout Paris, Rivera was known as the "Mexican cowboy," famed for his intellect, his ability to talk, his constant exaggerations, his wild behavior—and for his talent. Adored and pursued by women, Rivera was a spoiled little boy whose behavior at times was absolutely unpardonable. When he and his first (common law) wife, Angelina Beloff, lost their child, he never came home be-cause he couldn't face the tragic loss. He simply abandoned her. His fellow artists recognized his talent but could not abide his actions or his speech.

With his actions and his speech, Rivera wanted to exaggerate and shock. He must have been right at home in Paris, where for a hundred years the Romantic personality of French artists had taken great pleasure in shocking the public. There is, in fact, a French expression for this tendency—*épater les bourgeois,* to shock the bourgeois. The tradition of "épater" is at least 100 years old and is associated with the bohemian life of France's artists, writers, and poets. The term refers to the behavior of artists who made wild statements and committed irrational acts, not because they were crazy, but because they wanted to shock the people out of their self-righteous attitudes.

Rivera became part of a myth he created around himself. For example, he claimed that in 1904 he used to go to the city morgue looking for bodies of people who had died of violence—who had been freshly killed and were not senile. He said that he and his fellow art students lived on a cannibalistic diet for two months, and everyone's health improved. He claimed that he left this habit of eating human flesh, not out of squeamishness but because of the hostility with which society looks upon this practice. This story makes a point of Rivera's exaggerations. For the rest of his life, his reputation would suffer from his erratic behavior.

> **L**OOKING AT A CUBIST PAINTING IS LIKE SMELLING A LOVELY ODOR OF PERFUME," SAID PABLO PICASSO. WHERE IS IT? IS IT IN FRONT OF YOU? IS IT BEHIND YOU? IT'S ALL AROUND YOU. IT MOVES. AND IT'S THAT SENSE OF VIBRANT MOVEMENT THAT CHARACTERIZES A CUBIST WORK.

The years in Europe eventually took their toll on the Mexican artist, and the journey was turning into a crisis. Rivera described what happened to him at the British Museum: "I had again come upon my first love in art, the art of pre-conquest Mexico. I began to realize that in the heavy atmosphere of European culture I had begun to lose my bearings. Suddenly I felt an overmastering need to see my land and my people."

What Rivera saw at the British Musuem was something he had suspected but had never actually experienced. In the great museums of Europe, Rivera was exposed not only to pre-Columbian art but also to the codices. We know that as the artists of Mexico fought in the revolution and traveled around the country, they had a chance to see some of the art treasures of Mexico's past—pre-Columbian art in Teotihuacán and Chichén-Itzá. But in the European libraries Rivera saw the codices—books created and painted by pre-Columbian Mexican artists. These artists represented a high point of Mexican culture. When Spain made the decision to convert the Mexican Indians to Christianity, all of these books were stolen. They were taken out of Mexico and put into the museums and libraries of Europe. Here, years later, Diego Rivera came across the genius of his past. He says:

> Meanwhile, I painted, and although I now took some pride in my work, I was often depressed by a generalized sense of inferiority. It was a racial feeling, not unlike that felt by many artists in the United States and, like many of them, it finally would bring me to Europe. But in my case its roots were not specifically the same.

Before the coming of the Spaniards, the Mexican Indian artists had shown great force and genius. Like all first-rate art, their work had been intensely local; it related to the soil, the landscape, the forms, animals, deities, and colors of their own world. It was molded by their hopes, fears, joys, superstitions, and sufferings.

Under the rule of the Spaniards, the half-breed descendants of these great Indian creators turned away from the native sources that had given Mexican art its power. Feeling inferior to their conquerors and oppressors, they sought to raise themselves to equality by imitating the accepted models of classical European art—it was the response of men reacting to a tradition of defeat.

Rivera's words remind us of the history of Mexico and the humiliations of a conquered people. He was talking about himself as a human being, but he was also speaking for every Mexican Indian who had been denied a past, had been denied admittance into the present, and was therefore denied a future. He was speaking for every human being forced to cross the river and come to another country where, in the words of Octavio Paz, "even the birds speak English." When Rivera saw the codices, a sense of pride, a sense of accomplishment, a sense of himself began to take hold.

Sometime during 1918, the revelation of his discovery caused a crisis in Rivera's art. Modern art no longer held the key for him. Suddenly Rivera had the urge to go to Italy to study the art of the Renaissance. He spent two years (1918–1920) studying and making sketches of the works of the Italian masters. This is very unusual in the history

This handsome stone lintel, *left,* records that Shield Jaguar received his battle garb from his wife in preparation for battle in A.D. 724. Carved images of a feathered serpent, *below,* adorn the temple of Quetzalcóatl, one of many Aztec gods.

of art. It is not uncommon for artists to reject tradition and embrace the modern; it is highly unusual to reject modernism for the sake of styles hundreds of years old. What was Rivera doing and why? We don't know, and even Rivera might not be able to give us an answer. What do we know? What we can surmise comes primarily from our knowledge of the man, the spirit of his time, and his paintings.

CHAPTER THREE

ABOUT DIEGO RIVERA

When Diego Rivera was 10 years old, his family moved to Mexico City, where he enrolled in the Academy of San Carlos. The academy had some of the most brilliant art teachers in the Western Hemisphere. Founded at the end of the eighteenth century as the Royal Academy of San Carlos, it was the only institution in the country where the Spanish descendants *(Hispanos),* the Mexican Indians *(Indígenas),* and the people of mixed Spanish and Indian descent *(mestizos)* mingled freely. The tradition of San Carlos was freedom. Talent was the only requirement for entrance to the school.

When the 1810 revolution occurred, the San Carlos students were in the front ranks. After the War of Independence (1810–1821), Mexico emerged as an independent country and the Royal Academy of San Carlos became the Academy of San Carlos. The academy played a dominant role in the Mexican art of the nineteenth century. During the 1910 revolution, the art students rebelled again, not only against the injustices of a corrupt government but also against the influences of European art.

Years later, when Rivera had become a world-famous celebrity, he gave himself the name Francisco Pacheco. As Francisco Pacheco, he wrote stories he hoped would be read by young people around the world. One of his favorites was "The Merchant of Art." In this story, a young Francisco Pacheco was asked by a government agent if the school taught religious practices. The agent had hoped that the school would lose its funding because of its position on religion. Young Francisco, eager to defend the school's principal, told the government inspectors that the school did not impose

Self-Portrait, by Diego Rivera

religion on the students. Because of what he said, the other students called him a rebellious atheist. They constantly persecuted and totally rejected the little fat boy. The story reveals the isolation of the young Diego, but it also revealed much about the taste of the Mexican public.

Also in the story was Don Menjano, an artist who had gone to Europe and come back with the latest styles and knowledge of art. Everyone in Mexico was anxious to celebrate this artist. At the same time, many people made great fun of a local Mexican artist named José Guadalupe Posada. Posada, they claimed, was a fraud, not an artist. But Don Menjano was someone whom the richest society people asked to paint their portraits.

Rivera's story was a celebration of Posada, one of Mexico's great personalities. He had been

Calavera of Don Quicholte, by José Guadalupe Posada

Detail of *Dream of a Sunday Afternoon in the Alameda,* by Diego Rivera

Detail of *Dream of a Sunday Afternoon in the Alameda,*
by Diego Rivera

a painter, but he left the easel to create a new kind
of art, an art for the people—lithography. Each day
in the radical newspapers of Mexico, Posada's
illustrations carried intense social criticism and
wild publicity statements. His papers published
news of sensational events—trains derailed, fires
in the bull ring, collisions of trams and hearses,
mining disasters, women who gave birth to three
babies and four iguanas, a man with the body of
a pig. Posada illustrated the stories in a strange and
grotesque style. His most famous character was a
calavera, a skeleton that assumed a different pose
each day. Posada's illustrations represented the

José Guadalupe Posada caricatured General Victoriano Huerta as a huge spider crushing the bones of his victims.

Dream of a Sunday Afternoon in the Alameda, by Diego Rivera

conscience and the unfulfilled needs of the Mexican have-nots, the disenfranchised, those who went without land or food—the Mexican Indian.

While the government put many newspaper editors in jail for expressing their opinions, it dared not touch Posada. His work was so popular that it served the government's interest not to prosecute him.

As a very young man, Rivera used to visit Posada. Posada, indeed, became a major influence

on Rivera's politics and direction. Rivera compared the emotional force of Posada's characters to those of Michelangelo. Rivera said, "Posada knew as much about form and movement as any man I ever met. It was he who revealed to me the beauty in the Mexican people, their struggle and aspirations, and it was he who taught me the supreme lesson of all art, that nothing can be expressed except through the force of feeling, the soul; every masterpiece is a powerful emotion."

Years later, Rivera did a famous mural, *Dream of a Sunday Afternoon in the Alameda*. In front we see young Diego holding the hand of one of Posada's skeletons. The other hand of the skeleton is on the arm of José Guadalupe Posada. This mural was a fond memory nourished by Diego to celebrate the art of one of Mexico's unrecognized geniuses.

CHAPTER FOUR

THE SPIRIT OF
THE TIMES

The period between 1910 and 1920 was marked by the First World War and two Communist-inspired revolutions—one in Mexico in 1910 and the other in Russia in 1917. At that time, Paris was the intellectual center of revolution in both art and politics. The revolution in Mexico actually started in the year 1810 and was the beginning of a long, torturous road that led to the Revolution of 1910.

The Revolution of 1910 accomplished something that has rarely happened. Mexican artists and writers became the conscience of their people. They deserted their easels and desks to lead the battle for equality for the Mexican Indians. Many of them joined leaders such as Emiliano Zapata and Pancho Villa. Others began programs in mural painting. The mural is designed for the people in the street. The viewer doesn't have to pay an admission price to a museum to see it. The mural is there for everyone. Murals can be important political statements, and it is through the mural that the twentieth-century artists of Mexico became famous throughout the world.

The Mexican genius for art, especially for the mural, goes back centuries. It is found in Bonampak, in the churches, and even in the *pulquerías* (local bars). There seems to be something almost mystical in the way Mexicans respond to and make art. Some writers suggest that the strong and intense colors of the landscape are in the gene pool of the Mexican people.

As the artists of Mexico emerged, galleries and museums around the world sponsored major exhibits of Mexican art for the first time. During this

Triumph of the Revolution, by Diego Rivera

Man on a Llama, by José Clemente Orozco, *right;* detail of *Emiliano Zapata's Agrarian Revolution,* by David Alfaro Siqueiros, *below*

period, known as the "Mexican Renaissance," Mexican muralists became world celebrities. Artists like Diego Rivera, José Clemente Orozco, David Alfaro Siqueiros, Rufino Tamayo, and Juan O'Gorman took center stage. They became so important that artists came from around the world to be in their presence and study their paintings. Between 1920 and 1930, Mexico became a world center for art.

While most Mexican artists shared the ideals of revolution, they did not share the same beliefs about how to obtain fulfillment and equality. For *los tres grandes* (the big three)—Rivera, Siqueiros, and Orozco—there was no single enemy. Siqueiros painted the sufferings of the Indian population at the hands of a brutal, repressive capitalistic system. Orozco's paintings expressed a general sense of human brutality. For Rivera the real enemy was Hernán Cortés, who led the Spanish conquest of Mexico.

The word renaissance means rebirth. The Italian Renaissance had been a period of revival and

Self-Portrait, by David Alfaro Siqueiros (1945)

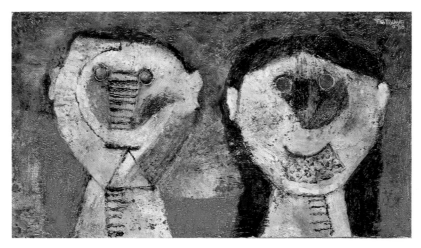

Dos Caras, by Rufino Tamayo

interest in ancient and modern learning, accompanied by intense artistic production. The word renaissance had its own meaning for the Mexican artist. The Mexican Renaissance marked the rebirth of pride in ancient Mexican civilization. The artists took pride in reproducing the images and celebrating the genius of that earlier civilization as a call for equality for the Mexican Indian.

Rivera was part of that world. Even though he spent five years in Paris, he began to take pride in his pre-Columbian past and to see his future as a Mexican artist. This meant a major change in his style. He wrote in his autobiography:

> My success as a modern artist was filled with discontent. I believed that life was changing, that after World War I [1914–1918] nothing would be the same. I saw a new society in which tastes would change. All these new modern movements, all these movements with all their subtleties—cubism, futurism, dadaism, constructivism, surrealism—would no longer be the function of art. A new kind of art would be needed and so logically I arrived at mural painting.

What did this mean? We can only guess that Rivera was redefining his life. No longer would he do "art for art's sake." The revolution had turned him into a revolutionary painter—compelled to paint for the masses. Yet the revolutionary painter spent two years studying the old masters of the Italian Renaissance in order to devote himself to his revolution. It is not surprising then that the young revolutionary painter should surface as the ambassador for the Italian Renaissance. His studies provided him with a profound understanding of fresco painting that would become his signature in mural painting.

In 1920 he came home to Mexico. His style had changed from abstraction to heightened realism. A good example of his new approach is his painting *The Flower Carrier,* a theme often repeated. In this particular version, the idea probably came from an ancient Aztec poem:

> I've come to offer you songs,
> Flowers to make your head spin,
> Oh, another kind of flower
> And you know it in your heart.
> I came to bring them to you.
> I carried them to your house on my back.
> Uprooted flowers,
> I'm bent double with the weight of them
> for you.

The Flower Carrier, by Diego Rivera (1935)

The flower seller bends under his flowers away from the woman, treelike but also crosslike, evoking the feeling of love and Jesus. The faces in the painting are simplified and flat. This is a Mexican painting on a Mexican subject, done with pride in the beauty of the Mexican landscape. Abstract art has been replaced by uncompromising realism. The bodies of Rivera's people represent monumental people brutalized by labor. The faces are general types, not individuals, and their skin is no longer European. Diego said, "The faces of Europeans had been clear against more or less dark backgrounds. In Mexico the backgrounds were luminous and the faces, hands, and bodies dark against them."

In 1921 Minister of Education José Vasconcelos asked Rivera to decorate the walls of Mexico's National Preparatory School with the mural *Creation*. This mural is not like anything Rivera had ever done or would ever do again. It is a strange combination of symbols, allegories, and signs. The subject is creation. On the left, Diego plants the spirit of woman, on the right the spirit of man. This mural was never one of the artist's favorites (he felt it was too Italian), but in its way it is a masterpiece of mural art. As you look at *Creation,* notice how the delicate rhythms of the hands and the placement of the figures guide the eye movement up and around the wall.

In *Creation* Rivera places the figures to fit the abstract lines of the wall they were painted on. For Rivera, the very essence of mural art is the realization that the muralist is an architect first, working and designing the mural in harmony

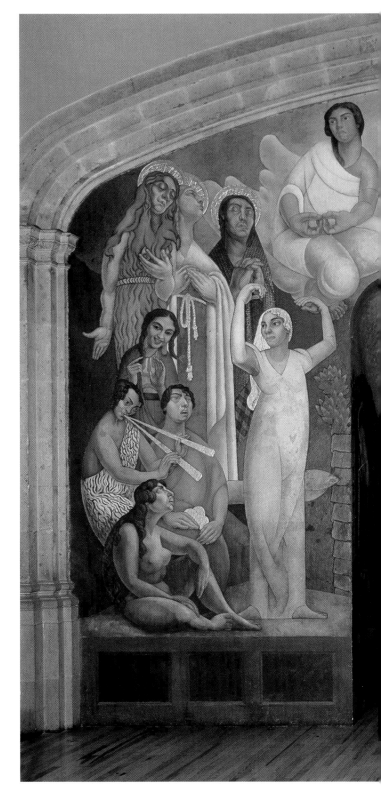

Creation, by Diego Rivera

with the abstract lines of the building. Notice the space Rivera has to work with. On both sides of the wall, his people are constructed like pillars, while the eye is directed by the fingers and the hands of the characters, the fingerlike formations of the clouds, and the rainbow life in the middle. The hand signs in the rainbow, in the center, are the ancient symbols of yin and yang, the male and female principles in Chinese cosmology. In the center is an open space with an organ. Out of this structure rises a hidden portrait of Rivera himself in a Christlike pose, surrounded by biblical symbols and animals. The painting is religious, but it is unique because the artist's characters are Mexican people dressed in the regional styles of the country. In place of Renaissance saints, Rivera substituted Mexican people.

The mural was very controversial. Not only was it the topic of heated conversations but the students started to riot and deface the painting. "Why," they asked, "did Rivera have to paint so much ugliness when he could have given us the beautiful women and flowers of impressionism?" Although Rivera was not satisfied with the painting, he was happy about the role it played in the new art of Mexico.

In its own unique way, the mural *Creation* reminds us of Michelangelo's masterpiece in the Sistine Chapel because of the way he uses the hands to move the eye across the curve of the ceiling as

Creation of Adam, by Michelangelo

the figures float in space. This sense of motion is one of the remarkable achievements in the history of Western art and very difficult to reproduce in book form. In the same spirit, Rivera's hand movements create rhythms that move the eye up and around the mural while his figures float.

Another echo of Renaissance style is the way Rivera gave halos to the angelic figures much like the Italian master Duccio in his *Maesta*. Rivera's years of preparation in Italy made him unique among the Mexican muralists. He had such mastery of Renaissance art that it will take scholars another hundred years to penetrate the hidden references and unexpected joys of this Rivera mural. There is in Rivera almost a hidden language behind a veil of concealments. The viewer who might not know Rivera's references can still enjoy the work. But the real pleasure of knowing a Rivera work comes from penetrating his scholarship and coming to terms with his meaning. A Rivera mural is worth precisely what the viewer can bring to it. What do we bring? We bring our knowledge of the past, our knowledge of art, and we try to make sense out of what Rivera himself was saying.

The more knowledge you have, the more you will find in the painting. Take, for example, Rivera's heartbreaking scene of the mighty hero Zapata in the mural in the Cortés Palace in Cuernavaca. The walls of an open, second-floor balcony corridor face the picturesque mountain valley. Here, Rivera laid out a series of incidents from the history of Mexico. Beginning with the depiction of human sacrifice in Aztec Mexico, the story moves along to the invasion by the Spanish, the oppression of the Indians during the colonial period, and their fight for independence, ending with the uprising led by Emiliano Zapata.

On the end wall, we see an Aztec sacrifice scene above the doorway. At either side, brilliantly

Emiliano Zapata, detail from *The Conquest of Mexico*, by Diego Rivera, Palace of Cortés

dressed Indians sweep across to attack the armored Spaniards. Another section of the wall treats the enslavement of the Indian. One scene shows the slave system on the sugar plantations in the state of Morelos, with the mounted foreman and reclining owner. The other scene shows the construction of the palace of Cortés under armed guards. The second wall represents the use of slave labor to build churches, the Inquisition, the conversion of the Indians, and the peasant revolution led by a handsome Zapata with a beautiful white horse. The scene is riveting.

There is poetry in the way the horse and rider seem to be looking at each other. There is a rhythm in their pose that demands our attention. We search our memory to inquire where we've seen this famous pose before. The source of this fresco is one of the most controversial murals of the Italian Renaissance.

When Diego went to Siena, Italy, he studied the murals of Pinturicchio. Pinturicchio had done a series of five murals commemorating the journey of Aeneas Piccolomini. In the first mural, the young Aeneas had set off to Rome, where he would later become the pope. For Pinturicchio that journey meant a painting in which everything was focused on the horse and the blessed voyage.

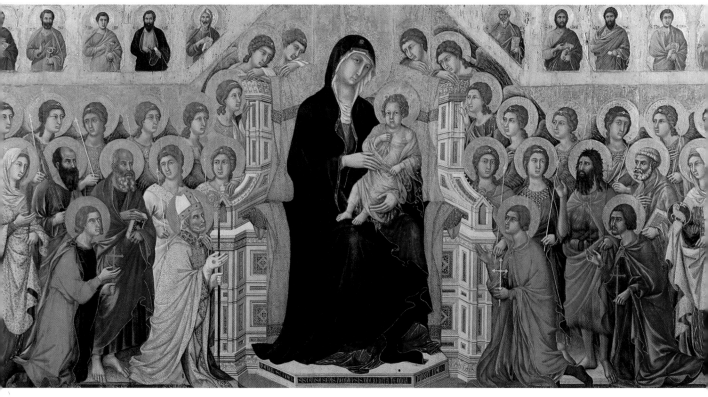

Maesta, by Duccio

In the mural, the horse and rider are surrounded by a storm, agitation, gropings, and confusions, but the horse holds our attention—so much so that when Italy's greatest critic, Giorgio Vasari, came to Siena, he said, "Pinturicchio could never have painted a horse so magnificently. It was painted by Raphael."

For 300 years, art historians and critics have tried to resolve the authorship of that painting. It has been established that Pinturicchio had received a contract for the murals. But we also now know that Raphael went to Siena to do a series of drawings for Pinturicchio's murals. So one of the great controversies in art history again became a central issue in Rivera's twentieth-century painting.

In the literature about the Spanish conquest, there is a tremendous emphasis on the role of the horse and horseman. The Aztec thought they were some kind of diabolic instrument of destruction. The Aztec were terrified of them. In the Cuernavaca mural, the Renaissance horse and horseman confront the masked Aztec warrior. Look closely at the detail. Renaissance artists painted horses with particular attention to the geometric formation of the horse. Ornamentation such as the steeled armor with the mask closed was used as a threatening decorative piece. The horse on Rivera's Cuernavaca mural is modeled after the prancing horses of Paolo Uccello's painting *The Battle of San Romano* (1432).

Detail from *The Conquest of Mexico,* by Diego Rivera,
Palace of Cortés

When Rivera lived in Florence, he spent hundreds of hours making sketches of Uccello's masterpiece. Painted in the style of Uccello, Rivera's Spanish horse and horseman are confronted by an Aztec eagle-knight wearing the mask and clothes of one of its animal gods. Here, Aztec mythology confronts Western technology. Rivera dramatizes

Crossing the Barranca, by Diego Rivera, Palace of Cortés. Bernal Díaz del Castillo relates how the Aztecs had closed all access to Cuernavaca. But Donna Marina, Cortés's concubine Indian wife, otherwise known as La Malenchi, plotted with other captive Indians to enter the city by climbing trees and fallen logs. It is now generally accepted that without her help, Cortés would have failed. In Rivera's portrayal of the event, soldiers are sprouting like bulbous fruit from the trees.

the moment by painting the Spaniard's horse in the style of Uccello and the Aztec warrior in the style of a pre-Columbian codex. For Rivera, the clash between the Aztec and the Spaniard was violent, and he expressed this through different styles of art.

In another scene, we sense the desperate struggle of the Aztec. Behind the eagle-warrior in the painting is an enormous horselike face. It is not an animal, nor is it a mask. It is a standard, framed to fit the shoulders of the Aztec warrior. Standards were worn like masks. In this case, the standard seems to represent the Aztec idea of what could possibly have been a horse. In other words, if the Spanish used horses to maim and kill, the Aztecs could use representations of horses to do the same.

Rivera knew that the Aztec warriors mounted standards around their shoulders when they went

Aeneas Piccolomini Arrives at Talamone with Cardinal Capranica, by Bernardino Pinturicchio (1502)

The Battle of San Romano, by Uccello

to battle. These horses are one more expression of Mexico's tragedy. There is something almost mystical about Rivera's treatment of horses. This is one more link in Rivera's relationship to the Renaissance artists. In the sketchbooks of Renais-

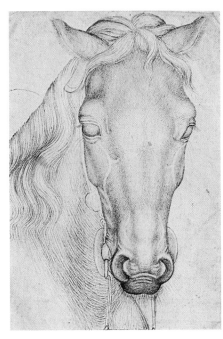

Head of a Horse, by Pisanello

sance artists, only the human form took precedence over horses in the expression of emotion and beauty.

Look, for example, at the entryway of Rivera's Cuernavaca mural. A foreman is mounted on horseback. He dominates the scene and directs the work of the sugarcane bearers. The curves of the horse, from a three-quarter view, join with the curves of the men who are bent beneath the weight of their burdens. The sugarcane also bends as it conforms

Detail from *The Conquest of Mexico,* by Diego Rivera, Palace of Cortés

to the arcs of the workers' backs. The horizontal and vertical lines convert this mural into a ballet of line and rhythm. The horror of the scene is reinforced by the ministers of the new religion, the forced labor under the sign of the cross, the burning of heretics, and the execution of rebels.

Zapata's horse seems the same as that of the Spaniards', but there is a difference. The Spaniards used the horse for domination. Rivera used Zapata's horse as a symbol of liberation. There is something very Mexican and very human in Rivera's horses.

Look at Rivera's *Liberation of the Peon,* located in the Secretariat of Public Information. The mural shows peasants who, after setting fire to a hacienda, free a peon who lies on the ground—almost dead—bound to a stake. Antonio Rodríguez says about this mural:

The Liberation of the Peon,
by Diego Rivera (1923)

Building the Palace of Cortés, detail from *The Conquest of Mexico,* by Diego Rivera, Palace of Cortés, *facing page*

The agitated rhythm of the mountains that serve as the scene's background, the masterful drawing of the foreshortened horses, and the ocher coloring of the landscape all harmonize to create one of the most beautiful and meaningful moments in Rivera's art. The rural school teacher who appears in the painting with a serene, gentle face and mystical gaze, with a shining book in her hands, is the messenger of the spirit who carries the new gospel to the countryside. Those who contemplate her, or listen to her, are imbued with faith. The soldiers, as men work to cut the ropes of the dying peon, they too are quiet actors in the drama.

Detail depicting human sacrifice, from *The Conquest of Mexico,* by Diego Rivera, Palace of Cortés, *below*

Self-Portrait, by Diego Rivera (1949)

This amazing work moves with the lines and colors of the landscape. But the horses are the vehicles of emotion. The agony in their gaze reveals the tragedy of the moment. Does the soft, cowlike gaze of the horses ring a bell? Suddenly we remember that those are the same eyes Rivera gave to himself in the self-portraits he often included in his murals. The distinguishing features include the soft gaze of a man who has witnessed much suffering and the touch of humor in the eyes that gives Rivera's work its humanity.

Rivera has been called a Communist. In some ways he was—in others, not. He did join the Communist Party as a young man. But Rivera knew about Joseph Stalin's treacheries in the Soviet Union and of the limitations set on artists in Communist countries. Artists had to submit to the judgments of the Communist Party, but Rivera refused to give in to Stalin's discipline. Because he refused, Rivera was expelled from the Party.

Despite his expulsion from the Party, Rivera remained true to communist ideals, which differed from Stalin's totalitarianism. Rivera became a spokesman for the persecuted, the landless, and the alienated. Only at the end of his life did he rejoin the Communist Party.

How ironic that this same artist became the darling of American capitalists. Some of the richest people in the United States—capitalists like Nelson A. Rockefeller and Edsel Ford—paid Rivera to do murals for them. When he painted the mural in New York City's Rockefeller Center in the 1930s, however, Rivera antagonized everyone by painting a portrait of Lenin, the first Communist Party dictator and an enemy of American capitalists, in the center of the mural. The Rockefellers became so angry that they had the mural removed. Rivera then redid the mural in Mexico's Palace of Fine Arts.

The United States offered to Rivera what Mexico could not provide, however. It brought together factories, scientific genius, and an industrial-mechanical age that let him produce art that could speak to the people who worked in the new soci-

Detroit Industry, by Diego Rivera, Detroit Institute of Arts

ety. When Edsel Ford brought him to Detroit to decorate the walls of the Institute of Arts, Rivera celebrated science and industry in his mural. He insisted that if his greatest paintings were in Mexico, his happiest days were spent in Detroit, painting the celebration of the automobile and the age of science that it represented. Rivera said that his style for the Detroit murals represented the machine age. But let's look at just one segment—

that phantasmagorical machine spitting out its materials. It is modeled after Coatlicue, a goddess represented in pre-Columbian art.

About painting in the United States, Rivera said the following: "The painting I did in Mexico in the 1920s had to conform to the peasant character of the people. But for me, I had to produce works in a highly industrial country like this United States."

CHAPTER FIVE

THE HISTORY OF MEXICO

Murals are not like other paintings, which can travel to other museums for exhibits. Murals adorn the walls of public buildings. In order to see most of Rivera's murals, you have to go to Mexico City.

His murals are even difficult to reproduce in books. The reason for this difficulty makes sense when you think about the problem: Rivera considered himself to be an architect first and a painter second. An architect works with three-dimensional images that the viewer must be able to experience (length, width, and depth). Since books are two-dimensional, reproductions of Rivera's murals lose some of their power.

With this said, we are now ready to mount the steps of the National Palace in Mexico City and confront one of the world's masterpieces, *The History of Mexico.* The strength of the mural's monumental proportions resonates from the enormous size of the wall. The mural dwarfs and dazzles the viewer with images never seen before. Approach the mural as if it were an impressionist painting. If you come too close you'll see only a maze of color and line. As you move back, the eye slowly focuses on objects and people.

The first thing you see in the mural might be the eagle at the center of the stairwell. This brilliantly colored eagle is the animal symbol of Mexico. Usually it is shown with a serpent in its mouth, but this particular image comes from an ancient Aztec sculpture known as *The Tiocalli Segrado (The Temple of Sacred Warfare).* According to the noted scholar Alphonso Caso, the eagle is a symbol of a holy war. (Caso was an adviser and consultant for Rivera's collection of Aztec art.)

The mural illustrates the history of Mexico from the pre-Columbian period to the present

Detail from *The History of Mexico,* by Diego Rivera, National Palace

time. On the right-hand part of the stairwell, the chronology begins with Rivera's portrayal of life in pre-Columbian Mexico—before the arrival of Cortés.

The scene centers on Quetzalcóatl—the plumed serpent. Quetzalcóatl was the god who, as the myth goes, was forced to leave ancient Mexico. His prophecy that he would someday return was keenly felt by the Aztec ruler Montezuma, who mistook Cortés for the light-skinned and fair-haired Quetzalcóatl.

In the mural, Quetzalcóatl is seen seated, instructing his community in arts and learning. He is in front of his pyramid temple, being adored by the white-robed Indians who kneel quietly before him. He carries a curved staff and wears an impressive headdress of green quetzal feathers. He is

teaching humankind to cultivate maize, to build pyramids, to carve stone sculptures, to create weavings, to express themselves by way of music, poetry, and painting, and to live thoughtful and productive lives.

Quetzalcóatl is said to have rejected human sacrifice and made human life pleasant. But because of this rejection of human sacrifice, the other gods did not act kindly to Quetzalcóatl. According to the myth, their priests got him drunk from the liquor of the cactus plant, and in this state he committed sins that demanded punishment. The price he paid can be seen at the top of the mural, where a serpent carries him into exile—to the Land of the Black and Red. At the top of this panel, the sun is upside down. A dragon comes out of a volcano spewing fire, and Quetzalcóatl goes off into the

Detail from *The History of Mexico,* by Diego Rivera, National Palace

Pre-Columbian Mexico, including the Aztec god Quetzalcóatl, detail from *The History of Mexico,* by Diego Rivera, National Palace

distance—ominous portents of a society about to be abandoned by its gods.

On the bottom half of the mural, Rivera shows signs of discord in pre-Columbian Aztec Mexico. He portrays exploitation and forced labor. A native with his hands raised complains bitterly about the way Aztec rulers have been treating the tribes. All this discord is a sign of what is to come.

Historians accept the idea that the small group of Europeans, known as conquistadors, would never have been able to conquer Mexico had it not been for the resentments of other native tribes against the Aztecs. The Aztecs captured other native tribes to sacrifice them to the Aztec gods. Rivera, even as he idealized life in pre-Columbian Mexico, never shied away from the realities of his people.

What is so astonishing about Rivera's mural is his extraordinary range of knowledge of Mexican art and history. The images he puts on the mural recount the myths of his people. What we are missing, of course, is knowledge about those myths. We might compare our looking at Rivera's mural without historical consciousness to looking at Michelangelo's creation of Adam in the Sistine Chapel without any knowledge of the biblical story of creation. We would lose much of the meaning. Not only does Rivera's knowledge of myth become an important part of the mural, but his representation of the Mexican natives is often inspired by representative works of pre-Columbian art. In Rivera's mural, the ancient work comes alive. This is a portrait of a country and a portrayal of its people, of their attitudes, their stances, and their faces. This mural is the spirit of *Méjico antiquo*—ancient Mexico.

As the eye wanders over the stairway, the tragedy of the Spanish conquest confronts the viewer. The conquistadors dress their horses in steel. These divine monsters shoot rifles and mortars made of hard metal that mutilate and decapitate. The conquest becomes the ultimate triumph of European technology. These Spaniards have sharp-edged swords and elongated spears.

The History of Mexico, by Diego Rivera, National Palace

Brave as the Aztec warriors were, dressed in the masks of their animal gods, they could not stand up to the power of gunpowder and steel. Although dressed in beautifully feathered tiger or eagle costumes, these warriors had no chance. The mural depicts heartbreaking moments in which we see unspeakable acts of human cruelty—Indians being reduced to slaves, and the Spaniards raping Indian women.

Rivera shows natives being used as forced labor to build new palaces and haciendas for the Spanish conquerors. The artist viewed these acts of barbarity as a true depiction of history. An extraordinary sense of suffering and defeat is expressed on the walls of the National Palace. Rivera confronts us with the worst forms of colonialism. He spared no one, not even the priests who came to convert the natives.

Detail from *The History of Mexico,* by Diego Rivera, National Palace

But he also introduces us to Fray Bernardino de Sahagún and Fray Bartolomé de las Casas, two Spanish friars. Sahagún was a Franciscan priest who walked barefoot throughout Mexico to convert the Indians. His amazing book on the habits of Mexican Indians is considered to be the first book on anthropology ever written. Although he loved the Indians, in his effort to convert them, he helped destroy their culture.

According to Rivera, when Las Casas came to Mexico, he tried to lighten the workload of the Indians. Suffering under the lash of the Spanish overseers, many Indians were dying. Las Casas went back to Spain and urged King Ferdinand and officers of the church to send black slaves to Mexico. Las Casas thought that the native Indians were not prepared physically or emotionally to withstand the lash of the Spaniards. He wrote a book in which he denounced the conquerors, the colonial landowners, and the church for the cruelty and plundering they committed against the native Indians. How ironic that good men with pure thoughts should produce such horrible results. This might be the artist's ultimate condemnation of colonialism.

As you look at the wall, you see 500 years of Mexican defeat, tragedy, suffering, and death—inflicted first by the Spanish conquistadors, then by invasions from other European countries, and finally by the corrupt Mexican governments. Just how Rivera planned the outline for this wall will be a matter of conjecture for the next hundred years. In his autobiography, Rivera tells the story of what happened to him and David Siqueiros while traveling on the ocean. He writes:

> An incident of only a few minutes duration had a profound effect upon me. Graciello Siqueiros (the wife of artist David) and I...were on deck watching the brilliant sunset. A glaring red ball suddenly bounded over the horizon of the sea and came to rest in the greenish-white bank of clouds. A few seconds

Detail from *The History of Mexico,* by Diego Rivera, National Palace

afterwards another sphere shot into our view, then still another. Siqueiros cried, "Look, Gracita! Look, Diego! These things are really small balls. If we get them in our hands, we could play with them. Real balls, I tell you." At that moment the conception of the National Palace stairway mural, which I had begun to plan and paint in 1922, flashed to completion in my mind so clearly that immediately upon my arrival in Mexico I sketched it as easily as if I were carbon copying paintings I had already done. The National Palace stairway rises broadly and majestically through a wide court, then forks at the first flight to right and left. For the wall on the right staircase I envisaged Mexico before the conquest. Its popular arts, crafts, and legends, its temples, palaces, sacrifices, and gods. On the central wall I would paint the entire history of Mexico, from the conquest through the revolution. At the triangular base I would represent the cruelties of Spanish rule and, above that, the many struggles of my people for independence, ending in the other arches in the lost war with the Northern invaders and the final victory over the French. The four central arches are aspects of the revolution against Diaz. On the wall of the right staircase I would paint the present and the future.

This is Rivera's analysis of his plan for the work, but other possibilities have to be considered. For example, notice how the sequence of images moves either from right to left or up and down. The technique follows the sequence of pre-Columbian codices, made up of glyphs and pictures which can be read from right to left or up and down. Look, for example, at the pages of a codex—in this case the codex Mendoza *(page 63)*.

Still another way of looking at the wall composition of the National Palace would take into account Rivera's knowledge of history, art, and mythology, as well as pre-Columbian art. For example, at a writers' conference a few years ago, the question was asked, "What makes this work so profound and so popular?" A scholar got up and said:

> Compare the murals of the Palace of Hernán Cortés or those of the National Palace with the murals of [Bonampak].... Indeed, the frescoes of Room Number 2 are remarkably similar to some of Diego's scenes, especially the so-called battles. There the similarity is so great that we possibly could have affirmed that those murals were his.

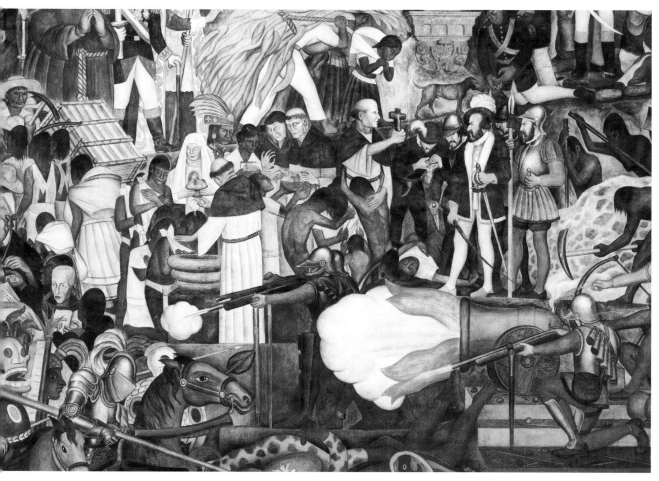

The Spanish conquest, detail from *The History of Mexico,*
by Diego Rivera, National Palace

The scholar recognized the similarities in composition between the Bonampak murals and the mural in the National Palace. This sounds reasonable, but it is preposterous. Rivera had started his history mural in 1930. Bonampak, however, was not discovered until 1947. How could the son of Guanajuato have known anything about the art of Bonampak? In the spirit typical of Rivera, his answer to this question was full of irony. He said, "Of course the works resemble each other; we're both sons of the same Mexican cactus."

Rivera also related a story of what happened when he came home from Europe unannounced. His mother was shocked and pleasantly surprised to see him. As the two were talking, Rivera's Indian nanny, the woman who had raised and

After the Spanish conquest, detail from *The History of Mexico,* by Diego Rivera, National Palace, stairway

breastfed him, came stalking into the house. She said that 12 days earlier she had had a dream about Diego returning, and she had come to see if indeed "her Diego" had come home. Diego's mother became quite upset and reprimanded the elderly Indian woman. But the nanny answered by saying to the mother, "You bore him, but I gave him life." In her milk flowed Indian pride and accomplishment. The Indian people had waited 400 years for Diego Rivera, their spokesman.

How can it be that Rivera's murals resemble the Bonampak murals he had not seen? It is prob-

able that by 1929, Rivera was able to paint murals deeply rooted in the Mexican past, based on his own knowledge of pre-Columbian art. He had already made exhaustive studies of the codices, the powerful art at Chichén-Itzá, and the sculpture and vases of the early classical periods. He had also acquired an important collection of art objects himself (now held in the Rivera Museum in Guanajuato). His life and work are a constant reference to thousands of years of Mexican tradition.

Like the composition in Bonampak, the mural at the National Palace is an enormous animation,

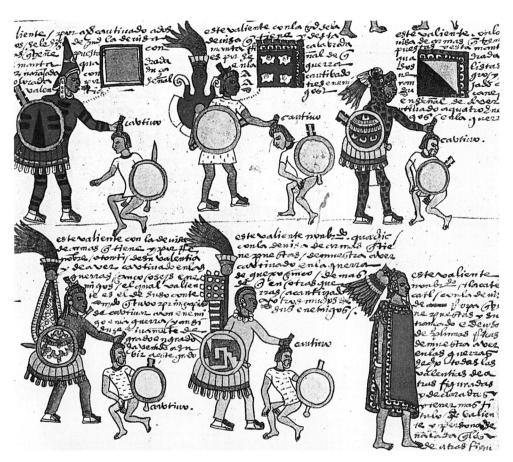

The codex Mendoza

almost a film. At the left of the central wall, soldiers are firing their guns. On the right, artillery men are making the gaping mouths of their mortars into fire flowers about to unfold. A figure is thrusting his terrifying lance in a diagonal direction. Another is throwing a deadly sling in the air. Aztec horns are sounding. Jaguar heads of warriors in their magic war attire rise in the air and light flashes. The mural is almost dizzying as motion swirls around the dynamic images. The viewer gets the feeling that the history of Mexico is one continuous battle of characters and terrifying images that passes from one generation to the next.

Rivera's mastery of the techniques of Renaissance art is important to understanding his work. One of the techniques he used is called the Golden Section. The Golden Section, also called the Golden Points, had its origins in the ancient geometry of Pythagoras, a Greek philosopher and mathematician. It is often given spiritual importance in paintings and architecture—especially in religious paintings and architecture.

The Golden Section is a very simple rule used for drawing lines and geometric shapes, particularly rectangles. A rectangle based upon the golden mean was considered a perfect rectangle because of the relationship between its length and height. It has also been called the Golden Ratio.

Based on theory of the Golden Section, here is the way in which the critic José de Santiago analyzes the composition of Rivera's mural in the stairway of the National Palace. The basic premise is extremely simple. It consists of diagonal lines that converge on eight golden points. Rivera uni-

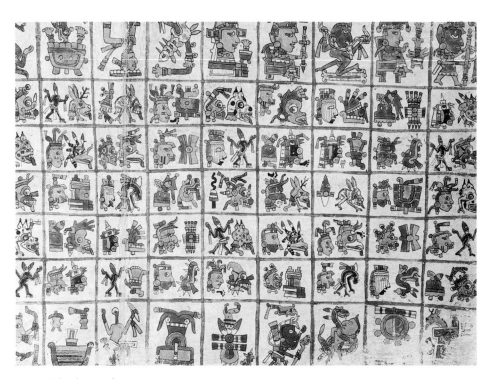

A pre-Columbian codex

Detail from *The History of Mexico,* by Diego Rivera, National Palace, stairway

fied the themes of the painting with modules, which correspond to the front wall and the two adjacent walls. The curved edges in the upper part of the modules are filled with landscapes and horizons, a technique Rivera used frequently. Crowded groups of people appear immediately below, but often we can only see their heads and small portions of their bodies. Nearly all of them are magnificent portraits, some full of irony.

From about the midsection, the inclusion of complete figures begins. This is done in such a way that the lower border has a great dynamic, an excellent sense of movement and harmony. This effect was evidently derived from Ucello's *The Battle of San Romano.*

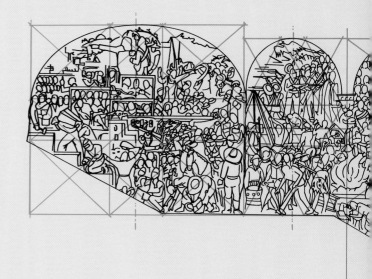

HOW TO FIND
THE GOLDEN SECTION

The length of the smallest unit is to the larger unit, as the larger unit is to the whole.

When this ratio is illustrated on a line, it looks like this:

A————————B————————C

When it is written in an algebraic formula, it looks like this:

$$\frac{BC}{AB} : \frac{AB}{AC} \quad \text{or} \quad \frac{\text{small unit}}{\text{large unit}} : \frac{\text{large unit}}{\text{whole unit}}$$

BC is to AB as AB is to AC

The diagram above shows how Diego Rivera probably planned his mural. If you look along the outer edge [of the diagram] of Rivera's mural, you will find some marks. These are called "the golden points." There are two golden points on each line. One is measured from one end of the line, and the other from the opposite end of the line. Rivera deliberately measured them out on the top and sides of each section of his mural. He then drew a line through the mural, connecting each point with its opposite point. Notice how these lines create a wide strip—or cross—in the middle of each section. Where these lines cross inside the mural, they create smaller rectangles on each side, and almost a square in the center. These areas are referred to as "the golden sections." It is within these areas that Rivera placed some of the more important people and images in his mural. Notice also that he probably drew a diagonal line from each corner to its opposite corner. Each of these diagonals passes through two of the golden points. He also drew diagonal lines inside the smaller rectangles and squares.

HOW TO FIND THE GOLDEN SECTION OF A LINE

To find the golden section of a line, you will need a pencil, a ruler, and a compass.

Step 1: First draw a straight line with your ruler. Label one end A, the other end C.

A————————————C

Step 2: Measure the line to find the halfway point and mark it with a tiny "x."

A————x————C

Step 3: With your ruler, draw a perpendicular line upward from point C, forming a 90-degree angle.

A————x————C

Step 4: Place the point of your compass on the tip of the C end of your line. Open it so the pencil touches the halfway mark (x) and swing it up lightly to make a small curved line (arc) near the top of the perpendicular line. Make this point D.

A————x————C

There are two golden sections on any line. You can find them by measuring from different ends of the line. You do not need your compass to find the reverse golden section. Just use your ruler to measure the distance from A to B. Measure that same distance from C. Make that point F. The length of AB=CF. Notice that this leaves a space in the center where both of the longer sections of the line overlap, that is, FB.

HOW TO FIND THE GOLDEN SECTION OF A RECTANGLE

Once artists find the golden section on two sides of a rectangle, they can project lines across the center space to create the golden section within a rectangle with four points.

If the artist draws a diagonal line from each corner of the rectangle, it should pass through two of the four golden points.

This is what Diego Rivera did as he measured out his murals. He decided to place the most important people and parts of his mural within the Golden Sections.

Step 5: Using your ruler, draw a straight line from point A to point D.

Step 6: With your compass still open to the half distance (AC), place the needle point on A, and draw a light arc on the line AD. Make this point E.

Step 7: Now put the point of your compass on D and open the compass so the pencil touches E. Keep this distance on your compass.

Step 8: Return to point A and draw a light line (the distance of DE) on your first line AC. Where the compass crosses line AC, make that point B. You have found the golden section.

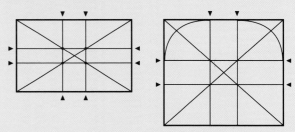

Detail from *The History of Mexico,* by Diego Rivera, National Palace

Just as important as knowledge of the Golden Section technique of Renaissance painting is the ability to see how works of the past come alive on the walls in Mexico City. For example, with knowledge of the works of Uccello or Pinturicchio, we can understand some of Rivera's meanings and subtleties. Great paintings and great painters have a special language.

It is not surprising that Rivera would take inspiration from Uccello. Uccelo was, after all, the Reniassance master of linear perspective. He was totally involved in discovering and applying rules of the illusion of depth in space. Painter and writer Giorgio Vasari tells us that Uccello eventually became forgetful and half-mad in his search for the rules of perspective. So intense was Uccello's preoccupation with perspective that he used to forget to come home for supper—or even to bed. Uccello's influence on Rivera was strong but not final.

Rivera was also a twentieth-century master with a thorough knowledge of cubist perspective. Remember, cubist perspective is based on simultaneity—that is, seeing the same object from many points of view at the same time. Both Uccello's *Battle of San Romano* and Rivera's *History of Mexico* have foregrounds, middlegrounds, and backgrounds. But whereas Uccello's lines create the illusion of moving backward in space and into the wall, Rivera's lines travel the height and move up the wall. Uccello's figures are portrayed from a single point of view, but Rivera's murals can be seen from all points of view—sideways, backward, up, and down. The diagram shows Rivera's techniques.

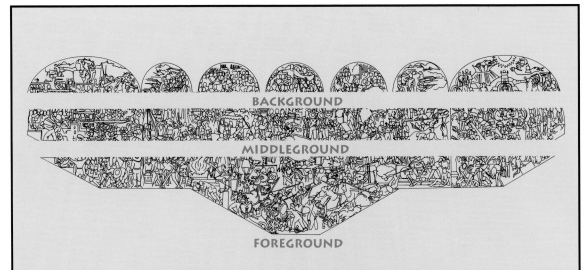

BACKGROUND

MIDDLEGROUND

FOREGROUND

A MATTER OF PERSPECTIVE

The National Palace murals have a foreground, middleground, and background, but they are not clearly defined since each panel consists of a layering of people and events. An imaginary line might be made to run horizontally along the lower third of the mural, beginning in the far left panel at the top of the first step and continuing above the heads of the people and the horse facing left. The line continues through the flames in the second major panel to the cannon flame and smoke, and it ends at the platform where the stonecutter stands, on the extreme right edge.

An obscured horizontal line in the middleground, or center third of the mural, might be drawn along the base of the five arches of the central panels. The lower two-thirds of the central panel is a continuous row of activity. The upper one-third is divided into five arched panels, each representing a separate story. The soldiers firing rifles on the left panel and those figures in the far right panel seem to be on the same level, which can be treated as a horizontal line. A sky and the tops of several structures appear at the highest edge in almost all of the panels.

The lowest foreground figures, at the bottom of the stairwell, are noticeably larger than the figures behind and above them. The figures move up the plane of the wall, rather than back into it—as is the case with Uccello's *Battle of San Romano*. These figures are seen from several points of view (typical in cubism) rather than from the single point of view found in the linear perspective of the Italian Renaissance.

Guernica, by Pablo Picasso

Rivera's relation to Uccello follows a rule in art. That is, great works of the past are reborn in the hands of great artists of the present. We see this dynamic again in another muralist of the twentieth century, Pablo Picasso. His work echoes the work of an earlier German artist. In Picasso's *Guernica* (1937), a cubist work, we see knifelike forms and recognize enormous suffering. Considered to be one of the masterpieces of modern art, *Guernica* shows images of a horse transfixed by a spear, a woman falling from a flaming house, a woman with a dead baby, a bull with its tail floating, and a dismembered swordsman with outstretched arms.

The Crucifixion, by Matthias Grünewald

Guernica reflects the horrors of war. The painting was done to commemorate the mass destruction and rape of the town of Guernica by the Nazis before World War II. As we look at this painting, we're not quite sure what we see except a general sense of anguish portrayed in images of despair.

What do we make of it? That depends again on what we bring to the painting as viewers. If you look closely at this work, you recognize Picasso's preoccupation with the crucifixion. As critics study this mural, they are quick to make comparisons with some of the masterpieces that might have inspired it—works from Raphael, Michelangelo, David, Reni, and Poussin.

The real center of the Guernica painting, however, is one of Picasso's favorite masterpieces, *The Crucifixion* by the German painter Matthias Grünewald. In Grünewald's painting, we see unbearable agony. But how did Grünewald convey this? Besides painting twisted limbs and countless lacerations and rivulets of blood, Grünewald did something that no artist had ever done before. He opened Jesus's mouth.

Picasso's *Guernica* begins with silence and death, but in the center—in sharp contrast to the silence—is the image of the horse shrieking (the open mouth). We look at the painting with our eyes, but the scream and the horror address our ears.

The teeth and tongue of Grünewald's Jesus are driven home more pointedly in the spiked, eloquent gaping of the *Guernica* horse. The cry of Grünewald's Jesus is sharpened and amplified by the radiating crown of thorns. These enormous points that appear in Grünewald's sixteenth century *Crucifixion* reappear in 1937, in the teeth and tongue of Picasso's shrieking horse.

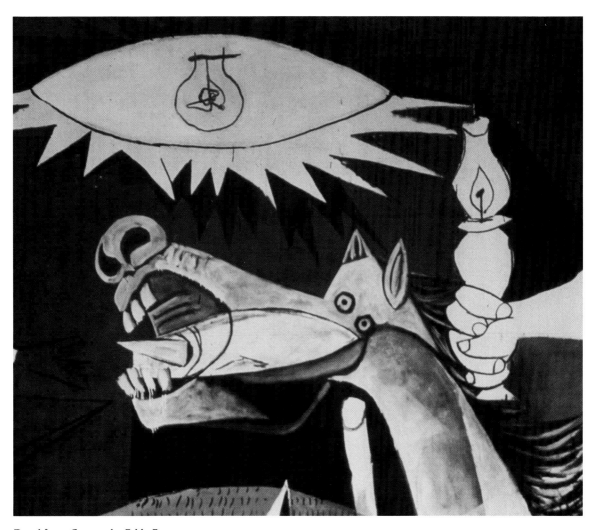

Detail from *Guernica,* by Pablo Picasso

CHAPTER SIX

RIVERA AS PORTRAITIST

Because Rivera's mural at the National Palace illustrates his vast knowledge of Mexican history, it will be studied for years. It would be impossible for most viewers to recognize all the people in Rivera's mural. But the faces on the walls of the National Palace reveal just how Rivera the muralist had become such an accomplished master of human portraits. In the spirit of his art, Rivera faithfully captures the physical traits and actions of his characters, as well as their personalities. He gives us a feeling of who they were and what they did.

Several representations of Cortés appear throughout Rivera's work. The one that holds most people's attention is that of Cortés standing near his concubine Indian wife, La Malenchi, while she carries their son on her back. Cortés is receiving tribute in the form of gold. At the same level, to the left, we see an Indian bound at the feet, hands, and neck. The Spaniards performed such acts of cruelty to the most rebellious Indians who did not want to work.

Rivera claims to have made an interesting discovery about Cortés's appearance after seeing drawings in the codices of Sajago. According to Rivera, scholars have proved that paintings of Cortés were a hoax, since this conquistador never allowed anybody to paint his picture. Rivera said, "The so-called pictures of Hernán Cortés, to which I also was one of the victims, having painted them in the Cuernavaca murals and in the National Palace staircase, are certainly modified copies of paintings of Charles V."

Rivera tells us why: "When Cortés was dying, in an act of contrition, the artist painted all his sins in the hospital portrait. He showed himself

Disembarkation of the Spanish at Veracruz, by Diego Rivera, National Palace

Engraved portrait of Hernán Cortés

as he was. However, his descendants had these paintings erased, even though there are definite remains of them. In fact, Hernán Cortés was short, hunchbacked, bowlegged, and ugly."

In this particular image, a man deformed by nature and suffering from syphilis is shown. In his physical appearance, the figure represents all the evil things Cortés was responsible for in the conquest—destruction, pillage, rape, and enslavement of the Mexican people. Here is Diego Rivera's enemy in full view.

Should a portrait depict a human being's facial characteristics, or should it reveal the character of the person? The art of portrait painting lies in the artist's ability to draw some profound truth about the subject, even if that truth is unpleasant. The portrait should leave the viewer not only with some insight as to who the person is and what the person looks like, but also with some sense of the person's character. The final image of Cortés represents the ultimate truth of portrait painting for Rivera. Cortés the conqueror is an aberration,

Hernán Cortés

a man driven by greed and the urge to destroy. When asked by Montezuma what it would take to make him leave Mexico, Cortés replied, "We Spanish suffer from a disease of the heart, which can be cured only by gold."

Rivera's portraits reveal the character of his subjects. For example, being committed to the war against slavery, Rivera could not forgive what he called Abraham Lincoln's "waffling" between freeing the slaves and saving the Union.

In 1933 Rivera painted a mural composed of 21 panels at the New Workers' School in New York City. Rivera's Lincoln is presented almost sleepily. Look at Lincoln's face. It contemplates with half-comprehending eyes the hanging body of abolitionist John Brown, Rivera's Civil War hero. Even though Lincoln has the Emancipation Proclamation in his hands, Rivera portrayed him as not understanding the complexities that John Brown did. Rivera's judgment of Lincoln is reflected in his portrait.

You begin to get a true feeling for Rivera's theory of portraiture in his painting of J. P. Morgan in the same mural. Rivera's Morgan is an extension

Abraham Lincoln and John Brown, *upper section,* detail from the New Workers' School mural, by Diego Rivera, New York

J. P. Morgan, detail from the New Workers' School mural, by Diego Rivera, New York

Sector from the New Workers' School mural, by Diego Rivera, New York

of his treatment of Cortés. According to Rivera, one of J. P. Morgan's first business transactions was the purchase of 5,000 old rifles, which he then sold to the government as new carbines for $22 a rifle. This shabby deal and his speculation in gold later in the war laid the foundation of Morgan's personally "earned" fortune.

Rivera has painted Morgan in all his "grandeur," with his right hand on his money bag. The theme is echoed in the lines of Morgan's bulbous nose. He is surrounded by rifles, while in the background we see the rifles exploding in the faces of soldiers. This was Rivera's judgment of what he called the evils of capitalism.

His portrait of John D. Rockefeller provides another example of his portraiture theory. Rivera had enormous respect for Rockefeller the oil baron. Rockefeller the banker was something else. According to Rivera, American involvement in World War I came somewhat as a surprise. The average American thought the United States would stay out of the war. But a group called the National Security League was organized in 1914. Its supporters included some of the wealthiest men in the country. Rivera's painting puts the burden of that war on that group of men.

In the foreground, Rivera has given us vivid portraits of the money kings. On the left is the mummylike face of John D. Rockefeller—ticker tape in hand. Across from him is French president Georges Clemenceau, who looks like a pleading dog, a mastiff begging for money. If you have sharp eyes you can locate King Albert of Belgium. Russian Czar Nicholas, with the face of an imbecile and degenerate, is in the center. In his hands is money, stained with blood. On the right is Clemenceau receiving money from the Morgan loans, and the mikado (the emperor of Japan), the appropriate ally in the "war for democracy."

Rivera viewed these murals, executed with great passion, as a gift to American workers. The portraits, which are sometimes caricatured, are faithful to their subjects and are extremely well done. Unfortunately, 13 of the panels were destroyed by a fire.

Detail from the New Workers' School mural, by Diego Rivera, New York

CHAPTER SEVEN

TENOCHTITLÁN

As the years went by, the achievement of pre-Columbian Mexico became Rivera's central passion. The dream of his old age was to locate and paint that golden moment in time when Indian civilization reached its high point, the final expression of its greatness. He recreated that world on the walls of the National Palace.

In 1944 Rivera prepared a fresco of life at the market of Tlatelolco. *(Refer to page 105.)* The market scene is framed by the great city of Tenochtitlán, the ancient capital of Mexico. In order to present this view with truth and historical perspective, Rivera spent years studying all the available texts, the artwork, the codices, and one particular book that is still read in awe and amazement.

Students and scholars, given the chance to read this book, are filled with wonder at the miraculous accomplishments of Mexican civilization. The book leaves the reader with the haunting question: if this was ancient Mexico City, why did the Spaniards destroy it? The book is *The True Conquest of Mexico,* by Bernal Díaz del Castillo. Castillo fought with Cortés and wrote about the expedition into Mexico.

Rivera read and reread the work, an eyewitness account of Bernal Díaz del Castillo. In 1945, after finishing all his research, Rivera painted the city of Tenochtitlán in the National Palace. Of all the works in the history of art, this particular mural has its place as the leading statement of a scholar, historian, sculptor, architect, and painter. In other words, this is the work of the complete artist. If there were one compelling reason to go to Mexico City tomorrow, this would be it. Once there, you would see and feel the life, breath, pulse, and dynamic movement of one of the world's great

The Totonac civilization, detail from *The Great City of Tenochtitlán,* by Diego Rivera, National Palace

civilizations. Before looking at the mural of Tenochtitlán, let us consider some of the words of Bernal Díaz del Castillo.

Castillo describes the pyramids, wide boulevards, streets of enormous beauty, and stately houses. He is amazed at the scientific knowledge of the community and the way the inhabitants used waterways as streets to get around the city. The descriptions are so powerful, Castillo's style so simple, that the reader is totally enthralled by what must have been a very high standard of living—higher probably than anything experienced in Western countries. The following are Castillo's words:

> The great Montezuma was about 40 years old, of good height and well proportioned, slender and spare of flesh, not very swarthy, but of the natural color and shade of an Indian. He did not wear his hair long, but so as just to cover his ears, his scanty black beard was well shaped and thin. His face was somewhat long, but cheerful, and he had good eyes and showed in his appearance and manner both tenderness and, when necessary, gravity. He was very neat and clean and bathed once every day in the afternoon.
>
> For each meal, over 30 different dishes were prepared by his cooks..., and they placed small pottery braziers beneath the dishes so that they should not get cold....
>
> While Montezuma was at table eating, as I have described, there were waiting on him two other graceful women to bring him tortillas, kneaded with eggs and other sustaining ingredients, and these tortillas were very white, and they were brought on plates covered with clean napkins.... There were also placed on the table three tubes much painted and gilded, which held liquidambar mixed with certain herbs which they call tobacco....
>
> Let us go on and speak of the skilled workmen Montezuma employed.... We will begin with lapidaries [cutters of precious gems] and workers in gold and silver and all the hollow work, which even the great goldsmiths in Spain were forced to admire....
>
> As we had already been four days in Mexico...Cortés said to us that it would be well to go to the great Plaza of Tlatelolco.... We were astounded at the number of people and the quality of merchandise that it contained, and the good order and control that was maintained, for we had never seen such a thing before.... Each kind of merchandise was kept by itself and had its fixed market out. Let us begin with the dealers in gold, silver, and precious stones, feathers, mantles, and embroidered goods. Then there were other wares consisting of Indian slaves both men and women...and they brought them tied to poles, with collars round their necks so that they could not escape, and others they left free. Next there were other traders who sold great pieces of cloth and cotton, and articles of twisted thread, and there were cacahuateros who sold cacao. In this way one could see every sort of merchandise that is to be found in the whole of New Spain....
>
> Let us go on and speak of those who sold beans and sage and other vegetables and herbs in another part, and to those who sold fowls, cocks with wattles, rabbits, hares, deer, mallards, young dogs...in their part of the market, and let us also mention the fruiters and the women who sold cooked food, dough, and tripe, in their own part of the market; then every sort of pottery made in a thousand different forms from great water jars to little jugs, these also had a place to themselves; then those who sold...honey paste and other dainties like nut paste, and those who sold lumber, boards, cradles, beams, blocks, and benches, each article by itself, and the vendors of ocote [pitch-pine for torches], firewood, and other things of a similar nature. But why do I waste so many words in recounting what they sell in that great market?—for I shall never finish

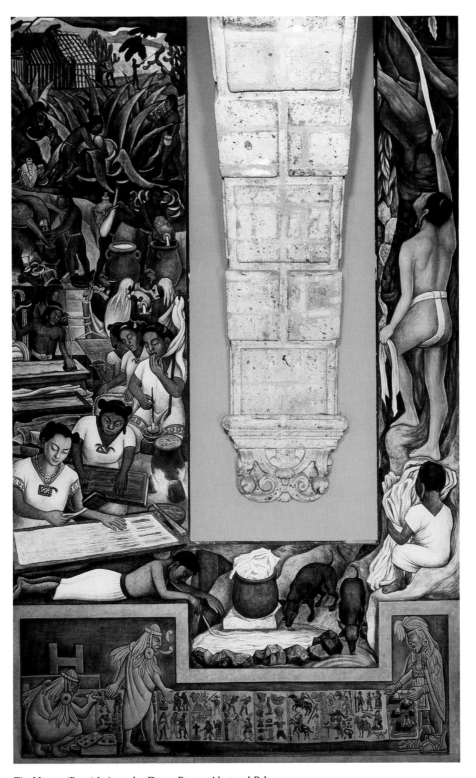

The Maguey (Paper) Industry, by Diego Rivera, National Palace

it if I tell it all in detail. Paper, which in this country is called amatl, and reeds scented with liquidambar...and things of that sort are sold by themselves....

I am forgetting those who sell salt, and those who make the stone knives...and the fisherwomen and others who sell some small cakes made from a sort of ooze which they get out of the great lake, which curdles, and from this they make a bread having a flavor something like cheese. There are for sale axes and brass and copper and tin, and gourds and gaily painted jars made of wood. I wish that I had finished telling all of the things which are sold there, but they are so numerous and of such different quality and the great market-place with its surrounding arches was so crowded with people, that one would not have been able to see and inquire about it all in two days.

With the words of Bernal Díaz del Castillo in mind, you are now ready for the journey into Rivera's miraculous vision of a golden moment that was and is no more—the moment that defines the purpose of our journey.

Rivera's mural of Tenochtitlán and the market at Tlatelolco shows the thousand-year-old civilized heritage of the Mexican people. The mural measures 16.2 feet by 32 feet (4.92 meters by 9.71 meters). Tenochtitlán is an aquatic city of enchantment, with straight causeways extended over the lake, against pyramids, temples, aquatic gardens, and two snowcapped volcanoes.

In the foreground, Rivera created a sense of life, and a sense of well-being. Here there is not only food for everyone, but human needs are being cared for. Everything here has order, law, and life. The best way to respond to this mural is by using Rivera's own words to guide us through the maze. Here is what the maestro says:

> This large mural represents a panoramic view of the Valley of Mexico with the capital

The Tlatelolco Market, detail from *The Great City of Tenochtitlán,* by Diego Rivera, National Palace

The Tlatelolco Market, detail from *The Great City of Tenochtitlán,* by Diego Rivera, National Palace

of the Aztec empire, the Grand Tenochtitlán, now Mexico City. In the center of the background is a range of mountains, including the famous snowcapped volcanoes Popocatépetl [smoking mountain], Ixtaccíhuatl [white woman], and several others....

In the center of the city are two great Aztec temples. Notice the left pyramid with two sanctuaries standing side by side on top of it.

The left one, with four vertical blue spaces... on each side, is to the rain god. The sanctuary on the right,...with four rows of five human skulls on each side, is to the war god. Note the blood running down the stairs from hearts sacrificed at the end of a year and...at the end of every thirteenth year....

On the right side is the pyramid to the Sun, with its stairs toward the west. It was surrounded by seven minor pyramids signifying the seven tribes from Aztlan that came... south in search of Tenochtitlán....

Here, too, on the right side can be seen the stadium where a deadly game of basketball was played. The captain of the defeated team lost not only the game, but also his life. Notice the interesting flying dancers' pole in the northeast corner of the ballcourt. Nearby is the zoological garden and a long detachable bridge which connected to the main pyramid. The city was crisscrossed with canals along which most of the capital's traffic passed.

In the upper right is the ceramic section. We see the crowds...walking through the pottery and food stands, men and women of different tribes. Some are...eating; others are buying kitchen utensils, bowls, *ollas* [round, earthen pots], charcoal braziers, incense bowls in the form of Tlaloc's (the rain god's) face, smoking pipes, plates, and artistically painted flowerpots. The Aztecs traded principally by barter.

On the same level line, to the extreme left, is the Calmecac College for the children of the Aztec nobles. The children were prepared for either the priesthood or military service, or they were apprenticed to merchants or artisans. Their outdoor play was carefully supervised.

On the lower part of the foreground is a group of natives trading reed and cotton mats.... With a lively expression of movement..., another group of Indians is off to market with a turkey, parrots, bamboo-cane, and long dry calabash gourds.

In the foreground, we see two farmers, father and son, carrying their wares to the city.... In the left corner, we also see Indian women selling fresh fruit, vegetables, corn, and different varieties of beans. Notice... [above them] some Indians who have different complexions. They have red streaks painted on their faces and cheeks and are from other tribes that came to trade with the Aztecs.

The hum of voices on a busy market day could be heard several miles away.

In the lower left corner, a child is carrying a papoose on her back and holding a bunch of white calla lilies. She is pulling a toy dog on wheels, an object often found in ancient sites. The toy clearly demonstrates that the pre-Hispanic people knew and used the wheel for ornaments and toys. The Aztecs did not use the wheel for transporting purposes because it resembled the sun god and the goddess of the moon, and it would have been a sacrilege according to Aztec religion.

On the same line, to the right, are more vendors. We see an Indian woman bent over, buying vegetables from a vendor wearing a rabbit's skin over his head. He is from the coast.

The Aztec noble in the upper, central section of the mural represents Tenoch, the founder of the city and the god of cleanliness. The cihuacoatl, wearing a jade crown and dressed in white as a badge of nobility, carries a fan of eagle feathers and rides in a litter. He is preceded by retainers whose duty was to inspect the markets and ensure the upkeep and

The Tlatelolco Market, detail from *The Great City of Tenochtitlán*, by Diego Rivera, National Palace

The Totonac civilization, detail from *The Great City of Tenochtitlán,* by Diego Rivera, National Palace

proper regulations of highways, bridges, streets, and plazas. Below the cihuacoatl are two guardsmen painted black in face and body. They symbolize the god of the night, Tezcatlipoca, or Smoked Glass. Wearing red cotton cloaks and jade earplugs, they are tax collectors.

To the left, a Totonac trader is paying tribute with transparent feather quills filled with gold dust. Below him are two Indian women using finger signs to trade, because they are from two different tribes which speak different dialects. On the same line, to the right, we see two other women. The one standing up, carrying the small round reed basket on her back, is of Aztec origin. The other, who is seated and has a Roman nose, is a Toltec. She is bartering a scoop of salt for tortillas. Above them we see two more traders. The one on the left, wearing a white cotton cloak...,

Courtesan girl with tattoos at the Tlatelolco Market, detail from *The Great City of Tenochtitlán,* by Diego Rivera, National Palace

Profile of a Mayan Woman, A.D. 726. Detail of a relief from Yaxchilán, Chiapas, Mexico. Note the imaginative rendering of Mayan practices and adornment, including the tattoos on the cheek and chin.

is a Tlaxacalan, and the one on the right, wearing a conical brown cap and a red cloak, is a Tarascan. They are bargaining through sign language. Both are chieftains of their tribes.

In the lower part of the mural, to the right, is a medicine man examining the mouth of a child. Possibly the man is a dentist. His wife, who is close to him, is selling medicinal herbs. In the same line, to the right, is a beautiful courtesan girl, Xochiquetzal. In her . . . hand, she is holding the native Indian flower, tigredia, the symbol of the goddess of love, flowers, and good living. She is surrounded by admirers. On the left side, Indian nobles are offering her a conch shell, a turkey, a magic flute made of human bone, and a jade necklace. Notice the winking evil eye on the old man. On the right is an Aztec general who offers, in exchange for her love, his prize trophy—the right arm of an enemy warrior, who was captured on the battlefield for sacrifice to the war god....

Next, on the same line but to the right, is the meat and seafood section, where we see wild deer, wild duck, frogs, and iguanas hanging.

Below this mural is an ornamental frieze... divided into five squares. The first, on the left, depicts the cultivation and harvest of corn and maguey. The second shows the harvest of carrots, pumpkins, potatoes, and plums. The third represents a religious ceremony dedicated to the harvest of corn. The fourth depicts picking cotton, then spinning and weaving it into cloth. In the fifth square, figures are cutting down strips of amatl bark; others are pounding maguey leaves to make paper or distill into hard liquor....

This mural is profoundly Mexican. All of the people are Mexican. Their attitudes and stances come from the thousands of pre-Columbian artworks that Rivera had studied. Frida Kahlo, Rivera's brilliant and beautiful wife, is represented in the mural. Several suitors are eyeing her, from the old man to the warrior who is carrying around a souvenir, in this case the arm of a Spanish soldier. Note all of Frida's feminine delicacies, including her tattoos, rings, and clothes. Also notice the human touches in the mural, such as the flower carriers, the child who is carrying a papoose and pulling a toy dog, the child at the dentist, even elderly women reading fortunes and giving advice to the lovelorn.

By the time we have gone through the market at Tlatelolco, we will have experienced a rich and active life. The mural's tone, exquisite colors, composition, and design have the softness and spontaneity of vibrant watercolor. The images are so alive with sight and sound that we can hear the buzz of the market. This Mexican landscape is the distillation of a fragrant city flowering in the fullness of its bloom. It is the quintessence (big word meaning "the essence of the essence of the essence of the very essence!"), the apotheosis (another big word meaning the ultimate expression) of the Mexican Zeitgeist—the spirit of the times.

While there is still much to be written about the meaning of Rivera's murals, the last word will always be his paintings. The next to last word has been written by the British anthropologist, Bronislaw Malinowski:

> Anthropology is the science of the sense of humor. It can be thus defined without too much pretension or facetiousness. For to see ourselves as others see us is but the reverse and the counterpart of the gift to see others as they really are and as they want to be: and this is the métier of the anthropologist. He has to break down the barriers of race and of cultural diversity; he has to find the human being in the savage; he has to discover the primitive in the highly sophisticated Westerner,...and, perhaps, to see that the animal, and the divine as well, are to be found everywhere in man.

> We are learning by the growing wisdom of the theoretician and by its complete dissociation from political affairs that the dividing line between the savage and civilized is by no means easy to draw. Where can we find cruder magic than in the political propaganda of today? Which type of witch-hunting or witch trial will not appear decent and reasonable in comparison with some of the forms of persecution of racial minorities in Central Europe? Cannibalism shocks us terribly. Yet I remember talking to an old cannibal who from missionary and administrator heard news of the Great War raging then in Europe. What he was most curious to know was how we Europeans managed to eat such enormous quantities of human flesh, as the casualties of battle seemed to imply. When I told him indignantly that Europeans do not eat their slain foes, he looked at me with real horror and asked me what sort of barbarians we were to kill without any real object. In such incidents as these the anthropologist learns to appreciate that Socratic wisdom can be best reached by sympathetic insight into the lives and viewpoints of others.

These words tell much about the art of Diego Rivera. His journey into style is a pilgrimage for humankind. His *History of Mexico,* although a history of one nation, is a history of all nations that suffered from the yoke of colonialism. His art, although a description of the past, is prophetic for the future. In his art, he spares the world—the haves from the illusion of superiority and the have-nots from the illusion of inferiority.

The Tarascan civilization, detail from *The Great City of Tenochtitlán,* by Diego Rivera, National Palace

EPILOGUE

The dates for the Mexican Renaissance are usually given as between 1920 and 1930. In that short span of time, one tiny country produced an incredible number of brilliant men and women. Their masterpieces rocked the world like a meteor falling from the sky. How and why this miracle called the Mexican Renaissance happened boggles the mind and defies human imagination. It was the moment of the Great Awakening with the revolution at its very center. *Viva la Revolución!* It was a revolution energized by artists and writers—*Vivan los tres grandes,* Rivera, Orozco, Siqueiros! Led by the genius of Diego Rivera, Mexico went in search of its roots and rediscovered its soul. *Viva Méjico!*

Emiliano Zapata, by Diego Rivera

FOR FURTHER READING

Arquin, Florence. *Diego Rivera: The Shaping of an Artist, 1889-1921.* Norman, Oklahoma: University of Oklahoma Press, 1971.

Mexico in Pictures. Minneapolis: Lerner Publications Company, 1988.

Rodriguez, Antonio. *Diego Rivera: Mural Painting.* Mexico City: Fondo Editorial de la Plastica Mexicana, 1988.

Wolfe, Bertram D. *The Fabulous Life of Diego Rivera.* Chelsea, Michigan: Scarborough House, 1963.

INDEX

Reproductions of artworks appear on pages listed in **boldface** type.

PHOTO ACKNOWLEDGMENTS

Alinari/Art Resource, N.Y., 40; Art Resource, N.Y., 14 (top), 41; Carnegie Institution and Pictures of Record, Inc., 11; c The Detroit Institute of Arts, Founders Society Purchase, Edsel B. Ford Fund and gift of Edsel B. Ford, 51; Florida Museum of Natural History, Gainesville, Fla./Stan Blomeley, 6, 8; Werner Forman/Art Resource, N.Y. 21 (top), 64; Giraudon/Art Resource, N.Y., 24, 32 (bottom), 33, 70-71, 72, 73; Independent Picture Service, 14 (left), 63, 77, 78, 79, 80, 81, 93; Erich Lessing/Art Resource, N.Y., 43, 44-45; Minneapolis Public Library and Information Center, 21 (bottom); reproductions authorized by the National Institute of Fine Arts and Literature, Mexico, 15, 16, 17, 18, 27, 32 (top), 50; San Francisco Museum of Modern Art, Albert M. Bender Collection, Gift of Albert M. Bender in memory of Caroline Walter, 35; Scala/Art Resource, N.Y., 38, 45 (right); Schalkwijk/Art Resource, N.Y., 2, 12, 22, 26, 34, 39, 42, 46, 47, 48, 49, 55, 74, 76, 82, 85, 86-87, 88-89, 90, 91, 92, 95, 96, 105-107; Robert Schalkwijk, 25, 28-29, 30, 36-37, 52, 54, 56-57, 58, 59, 60-61, 62, 65, 68; SEF/Art Resource, N.Y., 10.

PUBLISHER'S NOTE

Because murals are painted on the walls of buildings, they often show signs of deterioration from erosion, weathering, and abrasion. The surface on which the mural is painted also affects the clarity of the image and the sharpness of the color. For these reasons, photographs of murals sometimes appear to be blurred, and the quality of reproduction varies.

COLOPHON

The Journey of Diego Rivera was composed by Interface Graphics, Inc. in the Schneidler typeface with display lines in Lithos, printed by the John Roberts Company on Moistrite Matte and bound by Muscle Bound Bindery, Inc., in Minneapolis, Minnesota.

ABOUT THE AUTHOR

Ernest Goldstein, a nationally acclaimed art educator and author, was born in Boston, Massachusetts. He attended the Boston Latin School and Brandeis University. After graduating in 1954, Goldstein received a French Government Fellowship and spent five years in France doing doctoral work in psychological theory.

Since he returned to the United States in 1959, he has maintained an avid interest in education—particularly in the fields of art and literature. During the 1960s and 1970s, Goldstein combined two careers. He was a consultant to the Department of Health, Education, and Welfare's Bureau of Research, and he worked in publishing.

Both professions enabled him to visit classrooms and speak to students throughout the United States. His students range from preschool through graduate school. Because of his keen insights about art and people and his dramatic style of presentation, Goldstein's audience, no matter what age, is spellbound. His lectures have been described as "motivating, inspiring, instructive, and entertaining."

Some of Goldstein's other books include *Teaching Through Art, Understanding and Creating Art,* and a five-book series entitled Let's Get Lost in a Painting.